US ELITE FORCES –VIETNAM

By Leroy Thompson

Color Illustrations by Ken MacSwan
illustrated by Kevin Wornkey

squadron/signal publications

Combat Troops Number 7

Prior to rescuing ARVN POWs in the Mekong Delta a US Navy SEAL prepares to silently eliminate a Viet Cong sentry using a Smith & Wesson Mark 22, Model O silenced 9MM 'Hush Puppy' pistol.

ISBN 0-89747-170-9

If you have any photographs of the aircraft, armor, soldiers or ships of any nation, particularly wartime snapshots, why not share them with us and help make Squadron/Signal's books all the more interesting and complete in the future. Any photograph sent to us will be copied and the original returned. The donor will be fully credited for any photos used. Please indicate if you wish us not to return the photos. Please send them to: Squadron/Signal Publications, Inc., 1115 Crowley Dr., Carrollton, TX 75011-5010.

Special Forces Beret Badge

During October of 1968 Navy a SEAL waits in ambush along a trail in the Mekong Delta. He wears faded locally made tiger stripes trousers. The Olive Drab head scarf and the M63A1 5.56MM Stoner light machine gun are both typical of SEALs. (US Navy)

INTRODUCTION

WHITE STAR and Other Early Training Missions

There seems to be something in the American character or way of life that views the very existence of elite armed forces with a great deal of suspicion. And while elite forces are used during a time of war, and indeed often glorified by the media their very existence is underlined in controversy. Both in and out of the military there is constant criticism, and indeed even pressure to dissolve any organization considered to be an elite force within any of the branches of service. Regardless of how this controversy is resolved in the future, if ever, the elite forces did an extraordinary job in the past and can be counted on to do so in the future, when need rears its ugly head.

The peculiar nature and circumstances of the Vietnam War were such that it provided fertile ground for the growth of elite forces and the development of *special mission* tactics especially the Army's Special Forces. However, each branch of service had an elite special mission trained organization and the Army and Air Force had more than one:

Army	— Special Forces
Army	— Rangers
Army	— Long Range Reconnaissance Patrols
Navy	— SEALs
Marines	— Recons
Air Force	— Combat Control Teams
Air Force	— Combat Security Police

The Army's Special Forces, the largest and perhaps consequently the most controversial of all the American Elite troops can serve as a focus to introducing one to the elite troops belonging to the other branches of service. This is especially so since much of the tactics and training were pioneered and developed by the men of the Special Forces — the Green Berets.

During World War II the Office of Strategic Services (OSS) — the conceptual forerunner of American Special Forces — was active in Southeast Asia. However, the involvement of US Special Forces in Southeast Asia is traced to 1954 when a team from the 77th Special Forces Group (Airborne) was sent to Thailand to train Royal Thai Rangers. During the next few years members of the 14th Special Forces Detachment from Hawaii saw limited service in Vietnam and Thailand as trainers. Small training missions continued into the late 1950s when the 1st Special Forces Group (Airborne) sent personnel to South Vietnam from Okinawa. The South Vietnamese Special Forces were founded when the Joint Observation Battalion evolved into the ARVN 31st and 77th Special Forces Battalions in 1959. Members of the US Army Special Forces were involved in training these early Vietnamese special mission troops. A 77th SFG (Abn) team was also involved in founding and training the *Biet Dong Quan* (South Vietnamese Rangers) during this time period. In May of 1960 thirty US Special Forces instructors from Fort Bragg were sent to the Republic of Vietnam as a training cadre.

An important event for Special Forces involved in Southeast Asia had happened earlier in neighboring Laos. During the summer of 1959, LT COL 'Bull' Simons, later to win fame as the leader of the Son Tay POW Raid, took FC-3, which consisted of 107 members of the Army's Special Forces into Laos to train the Laotian Army in counterinsurgency tactics. Known as WHITE STAR this mobile training team initially operated in civilian clothes and *theoretically* operated clandestinely. However, in reality there was little secrecy about their presence or their mission since on their arrival Radio Hanoi had, in fact, welcomed them over the airwaves. By 1961 OPERATION WHITE STAR had grown to 300-400 troopers operating in US uniforms.

Perhaps the most important development resulting from WHITE STAR was the training of Meo hill tribesmen as counterinsurgency forces. Normally operating in half A-Teams (normally six men, but sometimes seven), members of the Special Forces trained the Meos into the most effective anti-Communist force in Laos. Under General Vang Pao the

In December of 1962 two members of Detachment A-14 inspect the punji stakes imbedded in a trench around the hamlet of Chau-Lang as part of its defenses. The trooper on the right carries a M1A1 Carbine. (US Army)

Meos would continue as the most reliable counter to the Pathet Lao for many years. In southern Laos the Kha were also organized into light infantry counterinsurgency forces and trained by Special Forces. These indigenous Laotian strike forces were the forerunners of similar units which the Special Forces would raise and train under the Civilian Irregular Defense Group (CIDG) program in Vietnam.

Theoretically, the US Army Special Forces was pulled out of Laos in October of 1962, as a result of an agreement reached in July of 1962 that all foreign military personnel would leave Laos. However, since the North Vietnamese Army (NVA) was blatantly ignoring the agreement, only a portion of the Special Forces personnel left. Many just headed for the Chu Porn Mountains and continued to work with General Vang Pao's Meos. Others went back to civilian clothes and worked in Laos on assignment to the CIA. At various times during the 1950s and early 1960s, Special Forces advisors in Laos and Vietnam ended up in civilian clothes as members of the Programs Evaluation Office in Laos or the Combined Studies Group in Vietnam. Either of these euphemisms could have been abbreviated CIA. While theoretically there as advisors and trainers only, members of Special Forces went on combat operations whenever possible. In February of 1962 for example, Special Forces personnel jumped into combat at Nam Tah along with the Royal Laotian 55th Parachute Battalion.

While they would not be deployed to Vietnam as a group until August of 1964, another important early landmark for Special Forces in Vietnam was the activation on 21 September 1961 of the 5th Special Forces Group (Airborne) at Fort Bragg. This early experience in Southeast Asia, especially the success of WHITE STAR with the Meos and Kha, and the establishment of the 5th Special Forces Group (Airborne) set the stage for the later intense Special Forces effort in the Republic of Vietnam.

Special Forces Training and Organization

To understand Special Forces missions and methods of operation, it is useful to have some knowledge of US Special Forces training and organization. Before undergoing Special Forces selection a soldier had to already be airborne qualified, and in many cases he was also Ranger qualified. Upon selection for Special Forces training he would receive intensive schooling in one of the following specialties:

COMMUNICATIONS: Sixteen weeks of training during which the trainee learned to send and receive Morse Code at a minimum rate of eighteen words per minute, cryptograhic skills, and the operation, repair, and maintenance of transmitting and receiving equipment, generators, and antennas.

MEDICAL: Thirty-seven to fifty weeks of Medical training during which skills through emergency field surgery and dentistry were learned. In addition to providing basic medical care to indigenous troops, their families, and members of his A-detachment, the Special Forces medic was also trained to teach hygiene and disease prevention.

DEMOLITIONS AND ENGINEERING: Eight weeks of training in demolitions and construction. Demolitions training placed special emphasis on creating explosives from available materials and the use of explosives for special tasks. Incendiaries, mines, and booby traps were also studied. Construction skills included dam, bridge, well and stockade building intended to aid in civic action programs.

WEAPONS: Eight weeks of training in both US and foreign weapons. About one third of the training was spent on mortars and another third on machine guns, rifles, carbines, and shotguns. The remainder of the time was spent on submachineguns, handguns, anti-tank weapons, grenade launchers, grenades, tactical training, building field ranges, and marksmanship training methods.

OPERATIONS AND INTELLIGENCE: Eight weeks of training covering tactical terrain, analysis, fingerprinting, order of battle, operational planning, photography, cryptography, clandestine communications, intelligence nets, methods of interrogation, organizing guerrilla units, and psychological warfare.

All specialties received training in techniques of teaching their skills. Normally, each man received cross training in at least one other specialty, thus allowing more flexibility should a member of a team be injured or the team be split.

The basic Special Forces operational unit was the A-detachment consisting of twelve men and was designed so it could be split into two six man 1/2 A-Detachments because of the duplication of skills within the A-Detachment. The A-Detachment was organized as follows:

Commanding Officer (captain)
Executive Officer (lieutenant)
Operations Sergeant (E8)
Heavy Weapons Leader (E7)
Intelligence Sergeant or Assistant Operations Sergeant (E7)
Light Weapons Leader (E7)
Medical Specialist (E7)
Radio Operator Supervisor (E7)
Engineer Sergeant (E7)
Assistant Medical Specialist (E6)
Chief of Research and Development Operator or Radio Operator (E5)
Engineer (E5)

Members of the US Special Forces inspect the remains of the village of Nam Qui during December of 1962. The large jars on the right were used in preparing *Nuoc-man*, the fish paste no Special Forces veteran will ever forget. (US Army)

The Civilian Irregular Defense Group (CIDG) Program

The success in training minorities in Laos, coupled with the need to deprive the Viet Cong (VC) free access to critical hamlets in the Central Highlands of South Vietnam convinced US and Vietnamese authorities of the advantages of implementing a local defense plan among the Montagnard tribesmen during the Fall of 1961. The *Yards* had traditionally been looked down upon by the Vietnamese who referred to them as *moi* which meant savages. The Montagnards were ready targets for the Communists who attempted to play upon both their distrust of the Vietnamese and their fear of the Viet Cong (VC).

To counter VC incursions, the *Rhade* (most prevalent Montagnard tribe) village of *Buon Enao* and its surrounding hamlets in *Darlac* Province were selected for a pilot Village Defense Program, which would evolve into the Civilian Irregular Defense Group (CIDG) effort. To help in civic action, primarily medical and engineering, a 1/2 A-Detachment of US Special Forces and some Vietnamese Special Forces — the *Luc Luong Dac Biet* (LLDB) — were first deployed to *Buon Enao* during December of 1961. This LLDB detachment contained a substantial number of Montagnards to help counter the Montagnard distrust of the Army of the Republic of Vietnam (ARVN).

By February of 1962, an A-team from the 1st Special Forces Group (airborne) along with an LLDB team had arrived to train these local Defense Forces in basic military skills and to help the villages establish defenses. In addition to small arms usage — primarily the M1 Carbine and M3 'Grease Gun' — building stockades and trenches for defense and basic defensive tactics were taught. At least one or two men in each village were given basic instructions in the use of a radio so they could call for assistance during an attack. A central 'strike force' received additional training and was more heavily armed, though it still functioned as irregular light infantry. This 'strike force' was a paid full-time unit which was available to react to attacks upon any village in their area.

By April of 1962, twenty-eight villages were protected by 1,000 village irregular defenders and a 300 man strike force. This number was soon raised to forty villages surrounding *Buon Enao*, and by August of 1962 some 200 villages in *Darlac* Province in the program with five US Special Forces A-Detachments assigned to training and civic action. Special Forces medics were especially effective since the Montagnards badly needed health care.

The program's effectiveness was soon tested at the villages of *Buon Tong Sing* and *Buon Hra Ea Hning* which suffered VC night attacks that were held and then driven off. By the end of 1962 *Darlac* Province was declared secure.

Because of the increasing number of Special Forces detachments being deployed to Vietnam; Headquarters, US Army Special Forces (Provisional) Vietnam was activated in September of 1962. Personnel from the 1st, 5th, and 7th Special Forces Groups were assigned for six month temporary tours of duty (TDY). So fast had the Special Forces commitment grown, primarily because of the CIDG Program, that by November of 1962, there were twenty-six A-Detachments in Vietnam controlled by three B-Detachments, and one C-Detachment.

B-Detachment

In 1964, for approximately each eleven A-Detachments in South Vietnam there was a B-Detachment to provide support to the A-Detachments. However, as the war progressed the ratio of B-Detachments to A-Detachments increased toward a theoretical norm of a B-Detachment for each four A-Detachments. Normally, a B-Detachment consisted of twenty-four men — six officers and eighteen NCOs — and was usually commanded by a Major. In addition to the normal specialties found in an A-Detachment, a B-Detachment included a supply officer and supply sergeant, an intelligence officer, and a preventive medicine specialist. An operational clerk was also assigned, though he was normally a fully-qualified Special Forces soldier who happened to have typing skills.

Members of Special Forces Detachment A-14 supervise construction of defenses at the hamlet of *Chau-Lang* during December of 1962. (US Army)

C-Detachment

A group of B-detachments was controlled by a C-Detachment, sometimes known as a Special Forces company. The C-Detachment normally had a strength of nineteen men — six officers and thirteen NCOs — and was commanded by a Lieutenant Colonel. In addition to the normal specialties represented in the A- and B-Detachments, a C-Detachment included a field radio repairman. Once the 5th Special Forces Group (Airborne) was activated, the theoretical organization was five C-detachments in the Group (one in each corps tactical zone and one assigned directly to the Group commander for special missions) with three B-Detachments to each C-Detachment and four A-Detachments assigned to each B-Detachment. Certain B-Detachments were assigned directly to special operations such as PROJECT DELTA or to training missions such as the LLDB training center.

The continued success of the CIDG Program made its continued expansion desirable. By the end of 1963 US and Vietnamese Special Forces had trained some 18,000 strike force members and more than 43,000 hamlet militia members. Beginning in November of 1962, and continuing through July of 1963, Military Assistance Command Vietnam (MACV)

(Above) Special Forces personnel and *cidgees* during an operation in November of 1965, which resulted in the capture of ten tons of VC explosives. (US Army)

(Above Left) An engineer of Detachment A-14 supervises the cutting of timber for construction of defenses at the hamlet of Chau-Lang in December of 1962. (US Army)

M3A1 "Grease Gun"

(Left) During November of 1965 CIDG personnel and their US Special Forces advisors examine captured explosives found in the hut in the background. (US Army)

Special Forces personnel of Detachment A-120 lead their CIDG troops back to *Vinh Khanh* after a two day patrol in the Mountains of II Corps during February of 1966. (US Army)

Special Forces medic of Detachment A-244 checks the wounds of a Montagnard woman rescued during OPERATION HAWTHORNE in June of 1966. Special Forces medics were trained specialists capable of providing a full range of medical services including surgery. (US Army)

Special Forces sergeant of Detachment A-412 at *Cai Cai* uses a Collins single side band radio to maintain contact with a patrol in VC controlled portions of IV Corps during May of 1966. The 'duck hunter' camo outfit worn by this Special Forces sergeant was widely used by CIDG troops during the early 1960s. (US Army)

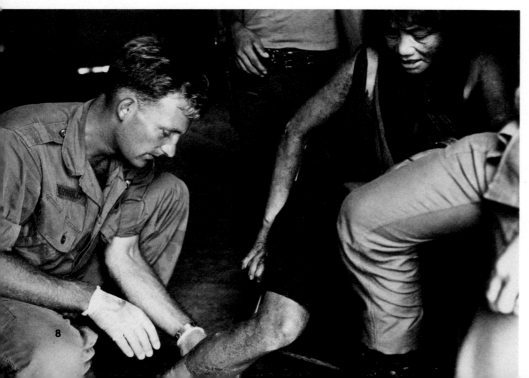

assumed responsibility for the CIDG Program as part of OPERATION SWITCHBACK. During this period, training for strike force troops was standardized at six weeks and for hamlet militia at two weeks.

The thrust of the CIDG Program began to subtly shift during 1963. CIDG strike forces began to patrol aggressively, searching out or setting ambushes for the VC rather than passively waiting for an attack before responding. In October of 1963 the Border Surveillance Program, which had started as the Trail Watcher Program, came under control of the Civilian Irregular Defense Group (CIDG). The Border Surveillance Program made use of Special Forces trained irregulars to watch key Communist infiltration routes along the borders of South Vietnam. This was one of the first examples of a change in concept for the CIDG Program. At about the same time, the Mountain Commandos, another irregular special mission unit, became the Mountain Scouts. Originally, the irregulars had been trained to protect their own villages, but as the program evolved into the later Special Forces fighting camps, encampments were established with military consideration in mind to control key areas.

By 1964 the area development aspects of the CIDG Program had taken a definite secondary role to the establishment of camps as fighting bases from which Special Forces-trained and-led strike forces could carry out offensive operations against the VC. As the CIDG Program expanded it was necessary to establish *strategic hamlets* in areas populated by other ethnic or religious minorities. In III Corps near the Cambodian border the *Khmer Serei* and *Khmer Kampuchea Krom*, among other groups, served in strike forces. The *Hoa Hao* and *Cao Dai* religious sects also furnished strikers, at least a few of whom had served in commandos under the French. The *Nungs*, ethnic Chinese, were also recruited into strike forces, often serving as camp security personnel as well for Special Forces compounds, an indication of their reliability.

During late summer of 1966 General Harold K Johnson, Chief of Staff of the Army, addressed headquarters personnel of the 5th Special Forces Group (Airborne). Standing at the far left is Colonel Francis Kelly, CO of the 5th SFG(Abn). (US Army)

Weapons specialists of the 5th Special Forces Group (Abn) fire an 81MM mortar at Nha Trang during October of 1966. (US Army)

An American Special Forces advisor of Detachment A-301 on patrol with members of the 324th CIDG Company twelve klicks north of *Tay Ninh* City in November of 1966. (US Army)

The traditional animosity between the minorities - especially between the Montagnards — and the Vietnamese often led to problems as CIDG units were turned over to Vietnamese control. At *Buon Enao* and elsewhere, the Vietnamese antagonized the strike forces and the hamlet militias, eventually leading to a rebellion by the Montagnards in September of 1964. Fortunately the US Special Forces — especially such officers as Capt Vernon Gillespie and Maj Edwin Brooks — managed to defuse the rebellion at many camps through the trust they had gained from the Montagnards, but not before some members of the LLDB had been killed or injured by the rebellious *Yards*.

Beginning in November of 1963, and continuing through 1964 priority was given to establishing CIDG camps along the Cambodian and Laotian borders where they could exert control over possible infiltration routes. By 1 July 1964 eighteen Special Forces A-Detachments and 11,250 strike force troops were committed to border surveillance. Throughout 1964 the need for strikers to garrison these border camps virtually eliminated the training of hamlet militia. The burgeoning Special Forces commitment in Vietnam necessitated the presence of a Special Forces Group by 1964, and in October of that year, the 5th Special Forces Group (Airborne) arrived to take control of Special Forces activities in Vietnam. At that time only ninety-five men were assigned to the 5th Special Forces Group.

In addition to conflicts arising from the turnover of CIDG camps to the Vietnamese LLDB, there were also conflicts resulting from the lack of aggressiveness on the part of the LLDB who did not want to go on night ambushes or patrols and did not like to operate with small CIDG units. As a result, while the Vietnamese Special Forces were theoretically in command with US Special Forces troopers along as *advisers*, these American *advisors* often ended up in command. In fact, it was not uncommon for a Special Forces sergeant to find himself in functional command of a unit large enough to be commanded by a captain.

Member of Special Forces Detachment A-321 and members of the LLDB plan a night ambush during OPERATION ATTLEBORO in November of 1966. The US advisor wears tiger stripes camouflage utilities. The scarves they are wearing were worn by many CIDG units in Red, Blue, Green, etc to distinguish units. (US Army)

(Above) A Special Forces demolitions expert prepares C-4 explosive for training purposes at the Tran Sup CIDG training center located six klicks northwest of *Tay Ninh* City. (US Army)

Special Forces Knife

Believed to have been made in Okinawa and issued to Special Forces in Vietnam. It had a 6 3/16' Blue blade and leather washer handle. The cast iron guard and butt is held with a brass nut. The scabbard is made of Black leather.

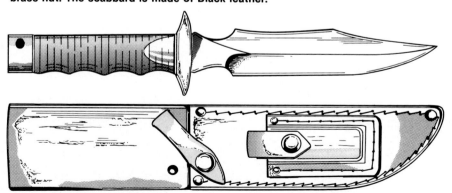

(Right) In November of 1966 members of III Corps MIKE Force, composed of *Nung* Chinese are being extracted by a Huey after heavy contact with the VC in the *Suoi Da* area during OPERATION GOLDEN GATE. (US Army)

Project Leaping Lena/Project Delta

In May of 1964 PROJECT LEAPING LENA was initiated. Under this project's auspices US Special Forces began training LLDB and CIDG personnel in long-range reconnaissance techniques. After the transfer of Special Forces Operations to MACV under OPERATION SWITCHBACK LEAPING LENA would become PROJECT DELTA, the first of various special projects carried out by Special Forces and indigenous troops. During its early stages only one A-Detachment was assigned to DELTA, although the commitment would grow until almost 100 US Special Forces personnel were assigned. As the importance of DELTA's covert reconnaissance mission grew, Detachment B-52 was activated in June of 1965, to control it. Under B-52 DELTA was organized into twelve reconnaissance teams (later expanded to sixteen teams) consisting of two US Special Forces and four *indigs* each. (Actually, each team consisted of four US Special Forces and six *indigs*, but on operations only six were normally deployed.) Six (later expanded to twelve) CIDG 'Roadrunner' teams of four *indigs* each, operated along VC/NVA trail networks dressed as VC; a *Nung* camp security company (also used for other special duties such as bomb damage assessment missions); and a Vietnamese Ranger battalion was used as a reaction force. The 281st Assault Helicopter Company was assigned to provide air support. These reconnaissance and 'Roadrunner' teams would carry out intelligence, hunter-killer raids, deception missions, etc, calling in the reaction forces if necessary to deal with enemy troops encountered. Early infiltrations were usually carried out by night parachute drop, but helicopter insertions and other methods were used later. DELTA was based at *Nha Trang* with many other important Special Forces activities.

PROJECT DELTA would remain active until June of 1970, and would eventually reach a strength of over 1,200 indigenous personnel assigned. In addition to carrying out their own reconnaissance missions, in September of 1966 DELTA was given responsibility for training US infantry as well as *indigs* in long range patrolling at the 5th Special Forces Group (Abn) Reconnaissance School.

Members of III Corps MIKE Force returning from a search and destroy mission during OPERATION GOLDEN GATE in November of 1966. Most members of this unit wear tiger stripes and carry M1 Carbines. Although this MIKE Force was a *nung* unit, the man in the mid-foreground wearing the green utilities and carrying a BAR appears to be a Montagnard or perhaps a Cambodian. (US Army photo)

Members of III Corps MIKE Force under attack by the VC during OPERATION GOLDEN GATE in November of 1966. They carry M1 Carbines which were standard for MIKE Forces and CIDG units until MIKE Forces received priority issuance of M-16s after the Tet Offensive. (US Army)

Members of CIDG Company 354 along with their advisors from Special Forces Detachment A-321 hit Landing Zone *Tien Thuan* at the beginning of OPERATION RENEGADE in November of 1966. (US Army)

(Above) A C-123 drops supplies to Special Forces Detachment A-101 at Khe Sanh in January of 1967. (US Army)

XM177E2 Submachine Gun

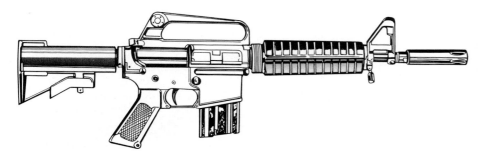

(Right) During March of 1967 a sergeant of Detachment A-301 gives instruction in the use of the M-79 grenade launcher at the Trung Sap III Corps CIDG training center. The well faded tiger striped 'boonie hat' worn by this Special Forces instructor was very popular among special ops troops as well as the *indigs* they trained. (US Army)

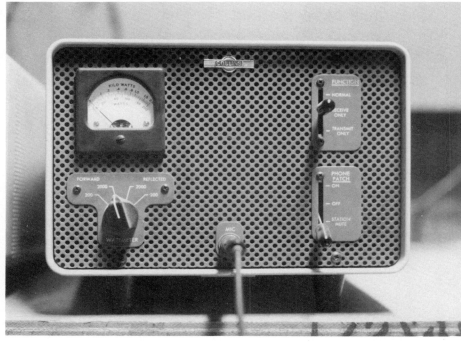

(Left) 32S-3 transmitter used at the Nha Trang 'Mars' Station to maintain communications with A-Detachments. (US Army)

(Above) Antenna of the Mars Station at Nha Trang as it appeared during late September of 1967. This radio station was used for communication with Special Forces units throughout Vietnam. (US Army)

(Left) The radio control box of the Mars Station communications system at Nha Trang. (US Army)

13

Formation of the MIKE Forces

As the CIDG program became more successful VC and NVA regulars began giving them more and more attention, mounting heavier and heavier attacks on their camps. In response to this, in October of 1964 the foundations were laid for the Mobile Strike Forces (MIKE Forces) which would come into existence in mid-1965. A Mobile Strike Force initially consisted of three companies and an HQ having a total strength of about 600 men, and was an elite element within the CIDG which could react quickly to enemy attacks on CIDG camps. Trained as airborne/airmobile troops, MIKE Force companies were not only used as a reaction element, but could carry out offensive raids, combat patrols, or ambushes. Since MIKE Forces came directly under US Special Forces control and were commanded by members of the US Special Forces rather than the LLDB, MIKE Forces could be used more aggressively and independently. Because of their combat ability and loyalty to the Americans, *Nung* tribesman were heavily represented in the early MIKE Forces. During June of 1965 a MIKE Force battalion was authorized for each C-Detachment, and one was assigned to Nha Trang directly under 5th SFG (Abn) control. In December of 1966 MIKE Forces came under joint US/Vietnamese Special Forces control, but until that time they had taken orders strictly from US Special Forces. Even after that date, for all practical purposes, US Special Forces retained operational control of MIKE Forces. The controlling Special Forces detachment for Mobile Strike Force Command was Detachment B-55.

(Below) During September of 1967 a UH-1C Huey 'slick' (transport) chopper lands on a mountain top landing zone to resupply members of the 5th SFG(Abn) and the 125th Signal Company who manned an important radio relay site. (US Army)

(Above) CIDG members at a camp in the Mekong Delta man a .50 caliber machine gun mounted on the top of the inner flood dikes built to protect the camp during the rainy season. This unit was advised by Detachment A-433. The Colored scarves are worn as a unit distinction. (US Army)

(Below) Members of a CIDG unit located near My An are manning an airboat which is used to patrol the 'Plain of Reeds' and interdict VC supply lines in July of 1967. This CIDG unit was advised by Detachment A-433. (US Army)

(Above) An Airboat patrol unit of the IV Corps MIKE Force prior to setting out on a patrol in the Mekong Delta during August of 1967. The tiger stripe camouflage utilities predominate, while the spotted pattern, often associated with the National Police Field Force and the PRUs, is seen only on the shirt of the man in the right foreground, who wears his MIKE Force insignia as a beret badge. The weapons mounted on the bow of the boats are Browning Model 1919 machine guns. (US Army)

(Above Right) A Special Forces instructor of Detachment A-503 instructs a Mobile Strike Forces trooper in proper parachute techniques at Nha Trang during October of 1967. This sergeant still wears the early 5th SFG(Abn) beret flash rather than the later flash which incorporated the colors of the Vietnamese flag. Note also the MIKE Force pocket patch and tape above the pocket and parachutist's and combat infantry badges worn on the breast of his tiger stripe camouflage utilities. (US Army)

Swedish K Submachine Gun
Sound-Suppressed

(Right) During December of 1967 a Special Forces advisor at Nha Trang supervises MIKE Forces troops in hand-to-hand combat training. (US Army)

Special Forces advisor test fires an M79 grenade launcher. (Larry Dring photo)

Special Forces advisor in tiger stripes and 'boonie hat' on patrol with CIDG troops. (Larry Dring photo)

(Above) Special Forces advisors on patrol with the CIDG unit they advise wearing typical field attire and equipment. An M18 smoke grenade is carried on the webbed gear of the man on the left. A Montagnard bracelet is worn on the wrist of the trooper at the right. (Larry Dring photo)

This Special Forces advisor on patrol with his CIDG unit wears a 'boonie hat' and locally made tiger stripes. A .45 caliber automatic is worn in a shoulder holster. (Larry Dring photo)

Special Forces advisor waits for an extraction chopper amidst purple marking smoke from an M18 grenade. The logs in the foreground are the remains of trees felled when the landing zone was cleared. (Larry Dring photo)

(Right) Special Forces CIDG camp at *Thien Ngon* viewed from the air shows the arrangement of the five pointed star outer defensive perimeter and a circular trench surrounding a five sided inner defense.

**Special Forces
Beret Badge**

(Right) This Special Forces fighting camp viewed from the air shows the inner and outer defense works pock marked with mortar pits. US Special Forces and LLDB usually would occupy the inner defensive positions, often with a *Nung* detachment. The arsenal and communications center would normally be located in the center. The outer perimeter was usually manned by CIDG troops.

(Above) Special Forces camp at *Bu Nard* advised by Detachment A-344 has defenses that included mortars that are backed up by 105mm howitzers.

(Left) This smaller Special Forces camp located with its back to a river illustrates how camps were usually constructed to take advantage of local terrain and the size of the defending forces.

(Below) The Special Forces camp located at *Ton Le Chon* has less sophisticated defenses than many camps but still has both inner and outer defensive perimeters.

CIDG Program at its Peak

The shift towards more offensive operations on the part of CIDG units coincided with the buildup of conventional US forces in Vietnam during 1965 and 1966. As a result, CIDG and other Special Forces trained indigenous troops often acted as scouts for US ground units and stalking horses for US airmobile units such as the 1st Air Cavalry or the 173rd Airborne Brigade which would be called in when the *cidgees* drew fire. Unfortunately, conventional US commanders frequently did not understand that the CIDG units were *irregulars* and had to be employed as such to be effective. The greatest contribution of the CIDG units — including DELTA and the later 'Greeks' (SIGMA, OMEGA, and GAMMA) — was in the area of intelligence gathering. As the value of their intelligence gathering was realized by MACV both the 5th SFG (Abn) and their indigenous strength continued to increase in order to fulfill the additional missions assigned to them, and by July of 1966 the 5th Special Forces Group (Airborne) strength stood at 2,627, and the camp strike force strength was at 33,400 backed up by 2,400 MIKE Forces. By October of 1966 there were ninety-seven Special Forces camps in Vietnam.

As PROJECTS SIGMA and OMEGA — special reconnaissance projects similar to PROJECT DELTA — got underway in 1966, MIKE Forces began to see increasing offensive action in response to intelligence gathered by DELTA, SIGMA and OMEGA. Among these operations were BLACKJACK 33 and BLACKJACK 41, the former of which was highly successful, inflicting some 300 VC casualties, due to the efforts of a mobile guerrilla force commanded by 'Bo' Gritz. BLACKJACK 41 involved a parachute assault by 373 members of the MIKE Forces and twenty-one members of US Special Forces on 13 May 1967.

BLACKJACK operations normally were the result of a MIKE Force recon platoon or a Mobile Guerrilla Force (consisting of a MIKE Force company and a recon platoon) being inserted and then reinforced by battalions of the MIKE Force to act upon the intelligence gathered or contact made by the recon troops. BLACKJACK OPS also included ambushing VC couriers or paymasters, destroying or boobytrapping weapons or food caches, and doing whatever possible to harass the enemy in his *safe* areas. Members of the recon platoons were often graduates of the reconnaissance school established at Nha Trang by members of PROJECT DELTA to train their own personnel. US Long Range Reconnaissance Patrols (LRRPs, pronounced *lirps*) were also trained at the MACV Reconnaissance/Commando (Recondo) School established in September of 1966, as an offshoot of the 5th SFG (Abn) Reconnaissance School, as were reconnaissance troops from Vietnam, Korea, and other allied countries. The three week recondo course included helicopter insertions and extractions, escape and evasion, survival, familiarity with the PRC-25, HT-1, and URC-10 radios, intelligence gathering including photography, long range patrolling, enemy weapons, and *other special subjects*. Normally, each class consisted of sixty students. Members of DELTA, SIGMA, and OMEGA teams were also trained at the facility, though not necessarily as part of the normal Recondo classes. Parachute training was also offered to those not already airborne qualified and in need of such training.

As of July, 1968, MIKE Force strength was divided as follows:

5th Mobile Strike Force Command assigned directly under the control of 5th SFG(Abn) — approximately 2,500 men in four battalions, one reconnaissance company, and an HQ.

1st Mobile Strike Force Command assigned to I Corps and controlled by Detachment B-16-1 — 463 men in two battalions, one reconnaissance company, and an HHQ.

2nd Mobile Strike Force Command assigned to II Corps and controlled by B-20 — 3,119 men in five battalions, one reconnaissance company, and an HHC.

3rd Mobile Strike Force Command assigned to III Corps and controlled by B-36 — 2,015 men consisting of three battalions, one reconnaissance company, and an HHC.

4th Mobile Strike Force Command assigned to IV Corps and controlled by B-40 — 2,199 men consisting of three battalions, one airboat company, one reconnaissance company, and an HHC. The airboat company assigned to 4th MSFC was necessary for operating in the Mekong Delta, especially during the rainy season.

Special Forces advisor from Detachment A-411 patrols the river from the CIDG camp at *My Phuc Tay* in IV Corps during the summer of 1968. He wears a 'duck hunter' camo shirt and tiger striped trousers. (US Army)

1st MSFC was based at Da Nang, **2nd MSFC** at Plieku, **3rd MSFC** at Long Hai, and **4th MSFC** at Can Tho. **5th MSFC** was normally based at Nha Trang but was used all over the country as the group commander needed them. By 1966 and continuing through the late 1960s, MIKE Forces were used in some of the most hotly contested areas in Vietnam such as War Zones C and D.

Throughout the 1960s, Special Forces continued to be involved in civic action and Psychological Operations (Psy Ops), but the primary emphasis was now on intelligence gathering and offensive operations. Combining both civic action and military advisory missions, Special Forces A-Detachment COs often advised local district officials and helped train the Regional and Popular Forces (Ruff Puffs) which came under the local official's command.

PROJECT DELTA continued to grow in importance as did other intelligence missions. By 1967 DELTA had expanded to sixteen recon teams, each composed of four *indigs* and two US Special Forces (though under Major Allen, the DELTA commander between 1967 and 1968 there were normally three US personnel on each recon team during operations), eight Roadrunner teams, and a reaction force of six ARVN Ranger companies. DELTA operations continued to stress the insertion of teams into VC controlled territory primarily to gather intelligence but occasionally to attack targets of opportunity. Other special operations had been carried out since January of 1964 by MACV/SOG, which will be discussed separately from the CIDG Program.

Another interesting Special Forces trained special operations unit which came into existence during the mid-1960s was 'Apache Force' which was made up of indigenous CIDG troops and Special Forces advisors who specialized in orienting US ground troops for operations in Vietnam. After orientation sessions, the Apache Force would normally accompany conventional troops on operations for their first few days on the line. The Apache Force evolved into Combat Recon Patrols which proved so effective during BLACKJACK OPERATIONS and in other aspects of the aggressive use of CIDG units.

By 1967, new CIDG camps being constructed were 'fighting camps' designed to withstand heavy enemy attack with pre-planned defenses in depth. CIDG night operations began to be stressed with a resulting jump in the number of enemy killed. No longer did the VC own the night. By 1967, PROJECT OMEGA and SIGMA had joined DELTA in full operation and were bringing in valuable intelligence. Though not a hard-and-fast rule, DELTA operated mainly in I Corps, OMEGA in II Corps, and SIGMA in III Corps. Because of close cooperation between US Special Forces and the Vietnamese Special Forces (LLDB), the LLDB began to show marked improvement during 1966 and 1967. Much of the credit for this improvement goes to US Special Forces Detachment B-51 assigned to the LLDB training center at Dong Ba Thin. Other B-Detachments in-country during 1967 included B-50 assigned to PROJECT OMEGA, B-52 assigned to PROJECT DELTA, B-53 assigned to ARVN airborne ranger training center, B-55 assigned to the 5th Mobile Strike Force Command, B-56 assigned to PROJECT SIGMA, and B-57 assigned to PROJECT GAMMA. It should be noted that PROJECT GAMMA was implemented in June of 1967, to gather intelligence about NVA bases and infiltration routes in Cambodia. Improvement in the LLDB was such that in 1967 it became practical to once again turn a number of CIDG camps over to them.

The Special Forces' plan for use of the CIDG during 1967 and 1968 foresaw the emphasis remaining on CIDG border surveillance camps and camps positioned to interdict the infiltration routes. Most camps built during this time period were assigned one or both of these primary missions. In the Mekong Delta, Special Forces fighting camps were often designed to be floating camps which could remain in operation even when the Delta were flooded. Aggressive patrolling by CIDG units in the Delta contributed greatly toward clearing the VC from the Plain of Reeds.

Early in 1967 Special Forces-advised CIDG units began operating from camps opened in war Zone C, which had been a notorious VC stronghold for years. Other heavily contested areas also came under CIDG control during this period as camps were opened where they would do the most good in the overall strategic plan for conduct of the war. Some of these new camps came under heavy attack by VC and NVA regulars. Two which withstood particularly heavy attacks during May of 1967, were Lang Vei and Con Thien. The availability of the MIKE Forces for rapid reinforcement combined with the availability of American airpower played a key role in preventing the fall of some camps. As previously mentioned, MIKE Forces were also used extensively for offensive operations unrelated to the defense of the CIDG camps. All MIKE Forces units, but especially the *Nung* ones, proved so effective, in fact, that between June of 1966, and June of 1967, Mobile Strike Force strength was doubled. MIKE Force companies had a normal strength of 185 men organized into three rifle platoons, a weapons platoon, and a small HQ. Though lightly armed for conducting operations in the rear of the enemy, MIKE Forces could call in artillery or air support as needed, depending on their location or mission. Normally, mortars, M60 GPMGs, and M79 grenade launchers were the heaviest weapons in the weapons platoon's TOE, though in certain situations, LAWs or other weapons might be issued.

To short circuit the corruption in the Vietnamese logistics system, the CIDG program and other Special Forces operations had their own logistics system based on forward supply points in each of the four corps tactical zones. Resupply for fighting camps was rapid, often using aerial resupply. The US Army Counterinsurgency Support Office, which had been established on Okinawa on 27 February 1963, took care of acquiring locally any special equipment or supplies needed by the Special Forces or their indigenous troops. Everything from rucksacks to special rations which were the forerunners of LRRP rations for CIDG and SOG recon teams to 'sterile' weapons passed through their supply channels.

A heavy weapons leader from Detachment A-244 looks on as a CIDG 105mm howitzer crew prepares to load and fire their weapon at *Ben Het* in November of 1969. (US Army)

In January of 1970 a group of Montangards prepare to move out of the Bu Prang Special Forces camp on a patrol. In November of 1970, this CIDG unit was converted to ARVN Ranger status. (US Army)

Two Special Forces advisors from Detachment A-242 instruct a CIDG trooper from the camp at Dak Pek on how to set a demolition charge in February of 1970. (US Army)

Special Forces camp at Dak Pek after being hit hard by an enemy attack during February of 1970. (US Army)

The Chopper pad of the 7th Aviation Company which served Special Forces. Detachment A-242 at Dak Pek under rocket attack from North Vietnamese regulars during February of 1970. (US Army)

A Special Forces medical supervisor of Detachment A-242 cleans the wound of a villager after an NVA attack in November of 1970. This medic wears parachutist's wings on his left breast. All Special Forces were fully airborne qualified. (US Army)

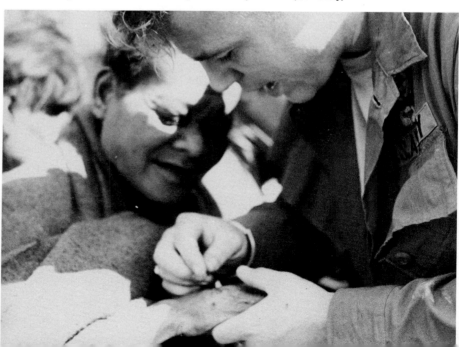

Tet Offensive

CIDG units, especially MIKE Forces and the Greek letter units, had proven their value at intelligence gathering and at wresting control of contested areas from the VC, and when the Tet Offensive hit the populated areas of South Vietnam on 29 January 1968 the *cidgees* proved themselves to be tenacious fighters in built-up areas as well. Fortunately for the government of South Vietnam some VC detachments launched their attacks prematurely against cities such as Ban Me Thuot and Nha Trang garrisoned by MIKE Forces which bloodied Charley's nose early in the Tet Offensive. Such important centers of Special Forces activity as Ban Me Thuot, Nha Trang, and Kontum were well-defended by members of Special Forces, *Nung* security detachments, and MIKE Force troops. OMEGA personnel also aided in the defense of Ban Me Thuot, and DELTA and GAMMA personnel were involved in defending Nha Trang.

Cidgees also contributed heavily to the defense of Qui Nhon, Pleiku, Chau Doc, Phan Thiet, and Dalat. Pleiku was the base for Detachment C-2 and the 2nd Mobile Strike Force Command, while Chau Doc was the base for Detachment B-42 with its attached irregulars. Each of the other cities had Special Forces and irregulars based in their environs or nearby.

During the build-up for the Tet Offensive and during it, most of the CIDG camps other than those in I Corps were left alone as VC strength was concentrated around Khe Sanh. However some Special Forces camps came under attack, particularly Lang Vei under Detachment A-101. Lang Vei's history had been an active one, since its establishment in December of 1966. On 4 May 1967, the camp had been virtually destroyed in an attack aided by VC who had infiltrated the CIDG units in the camp. Finally, on 7 February 1968 the camp was overrun by enemy forces which included NVA tanks.

As the VC remnants, who had survived the assaults on the cities, retreated after Tet, CIDG units punished them severely by striking them along their infiltration/exfiltration routes.

The excellent performance of the *cidgees* during Tet caused certain changes in the way they were viewed by MACV and the South Vietnamese military hierarchy. CIDG units were given greater responsibility in defending II, III, and IV Corps as conventional ARVN units were moved into I Corps to resecure areas occupied by the VC and NVA during the Tet Offensive. As a result of their good showing, in April of 1968 CIDG units were given priority in weapons modernization as they received M-16 assault rifles, M-60 GPMGs, and M-79 grenade launchers.

MIKE Force strength was also greatly increased. By the summer of 1968, there were thirty-four MIKE Force companies — five in I Corps (Da Nang), twelve in II Corps (*Pleiku, Ban Me Thuot, Kontum,* and *Qui Nhon*), seven in III Corps (*Lang Hai*), and ten in IV Corps (*Dan Phuc, Moc Hoa, To Chau,* an *Cao Lanh*). By the fall of 1968, 5th Special Forces Group strength was over 3,500 with over 27,000 CIDG and over 7,000 MIKE Force personnel under their supervision.

Vietnamization

Beginning early in 1968 the process of turning over CIDG camps to Vietnamese control was speeded up. MACV also developed the concept of using CIDG personnel primarily along the western borders of Vietnam to interdict infiltration routes. More and more responsibility, from C-Detachment down through A-Detachment level, was turned over to the LLDB to prepare them for the eventual complete turn-over of the CIDG program. Emphasis was also placed on turning over civic action and Psy Ops to the Vietnamese.

During 1969 as the LLDB became more competent, turnover of the strategically important border surveillance and interdiction camps to South Vietnamese control began. Nevertheless, US Special Forces strength in Vietnam peaked during 1969, with over 4,000

(Above) At Dak Pek during June of 1970 Special Forces ordnance experts of Detachment A29 prepare to burn small arms ammunition with diesel fuel. (US Army)

Special Forces troopers assigned (including those on special operations such as SOG). By early 1970, in fact, it had been decided to end the CIDG program and to absorb CIDG units into the Army of the Republic of Vietnam. As a result during the fall of 1970 a few camps were closed down, and thirty-seven were converted to ARVN Ranger camps with their CIDG complement becoming ARVN Ranger battalions, primarily 'Border Rangers'. As Special Forces responsibilities were terminated the 5th Special Forces Group (Airborne) strength began to decline, dropping to under 3,000 by late 1970.

During 1970 CIDG units along with members of US Special Forces participated in operations in Cambodia between 29 April and 30 June 1970. CIDG companies from *Duc Hue* and *Tra Cu* played an especially important role in Cambodia as they assaulted a VC training area and discovered large caches of crew served weapons and other equipment.

On 31 December 1970, participation of the 5th SFG (Abn) in the CIDG Program officially terminated. On 3 March 1971 the 5th SFG(Abn) officially departed Vietnam for Fort Bragg, although some Special Forces troopers assigned to advisory missions or special operations would remain much longer. During the 1972 Communist Easter Offensive, a limited number of Special Forces personnel who had previously served in Vietnam returned for temporary duty. As in the early days of Special Forces involvement in Vietnam, Special Forces personnel were reportedly assigned to the CIA and operating in-country during the final days before the fall of South Vietnam.

Special Forces instructor of Detachment B-51 at the basic airborne school at *Dong Ba Thin* briefs trainees prior to the mock door phase of their training. May 1970. (US Army)

(Left) Two members of USAF's Combat Control Team (CCT) direct an incoming transport aircraft at the landing strip of a Special Forces camp during August of 1968.

(Right) During early 1963 a US Army Ranger advisor to the ARVN Rangers uses his Randall Attack/Survival Knife to cut the ignition cord for an M18A1 Claymore mine while instructing the kneeling BDQ in the use of this device.

(Above) US LRRP of Company N, 75th Infantry (Ranger), 173rd Airborne Brigade checks a shotgun shell before loading it into his Ithaca shotgun prior to a mission during March of 1971. His captured Tokarev M-51 pistol is worn in a makeshift holster originally intended for a S&W .38 caliber Special revolver.

(Above Right) LRRP of Company F, 58th Infantry (Long Range Patrol), 101st Airborne Division on patrol during June of 1968 in *Thua Thien* Province as part of OPERATION NEVADA EAGLE. The pocket patch worn on the left pocket identifies him as a graduate of the MACV Recondo School at *Nha Trang*. His M-16 rifle mounts an AN/PVS-2 starlight scope, possibly indicating his assignment to a night ambush team.

(Right) Two Special Forces recon troopers assigned to 'PROJECT DELTA' are being extracted via STABO rig during an operation late in 1969.

(Above) Son Tay Raider on 21 November 1970 prepares to move through a doorway in the prison compound. His XM177E2 has an Aimpoint sight taped to the carry handle. These sights were acquired from private sources since there was not a satisfactory lightweight sight of this type in the Army logistics system.

(Above) A US Special Forces NCO assigned to a MACV/SOG Recon Team in Command Control Central (CCC) is alert to the possible presence of the enemy while on a reconnaissance mission into Cambodia during April of 1970, prior to the 'incursion' into that country. His weapon is a suppressed Swedish 'K' SMG, and he wears a STABO rig for helicopter extraction.

(Right) During November of 1964, a Special Forces captain instructs a Montagnard Strike Force member in the procedure for loading the M3A1 'Grease Gun'. The Special Forces officer wears a Randall fighting knife on his hip, and a Rolex watch, one of the most prized possessions in Vietnam, on his wrist.

MACV/SOG

Separate from 'conventional', *unconventional operations* of the 5th Special Forces Group were the clandestine operations of Military Assistance Command Vietnam/Studies and Observations Group (MACV/SOG). The Studies and Observations Group (SOG) was a cover name to disguise SOG's real function, and the name 'Special Operations Group', as it was sometimes called, described its real mission more accurately.

Activated in January of 1964, SOG was a joint services unit composed of members from all four branches of the armed forces, including Navy SEALs, Marine Recons, Air Force special operations pilots of the 90th Special Operations Wing, but predominantly Army Special Forces. Naval craft were made available for clandestine insertions into North Vietnam. Assigned to MACV/SOG, Navy SEALs reportedly became most familiar with Haiphong Harbor. Working closely with the CIA, SOG carried out clandestine operations all over Southeast Asia, and although supervised by MACV, SOG came directly under control of the Joint Chiefs of Staff through the Special Assistant for Counterinsurgency and Special Activities. Among other duties, SOG worked closely with the Vietnamese Special Exploitation Service (SES), which became the Strategic Technical Directorate in September of 1967, to carry out sabotage, Psy Ops, intelligence, and other *special missions*. Among the many excellent officers assigned to SOG were Colonel Donald Blackburn (who in World War II had led a Philippine guerrilla unit known as 'Blackburn's Headhunters') and Colonel John Singlaub, both commanders of MACV/SOG, and Colonel 'Bull' Simons who commanded CPS 35 under Blackburn and organized many of the covert missions into Laos (where he had earlier worked as CO of WHITE STAR), Cambodia, and North Vietnam.

At its peak, MACV/SOG had some 2,000 Americans and over 8,000 *indigs* assigned. A larger percentage of the Americans were Special Forces personnel whose assignment to SOG was covered by assignment to a 5th SFG (Abn) unit euphemistically known as Special Operations Augmentation. Many members of the 1st SFG (Abn) on Okinawa volunteered for TDY tours with SOG as did a substantial number of men from the 7th SFG(Abn).

MACV/SOG's missions included: cross border operations into Cambodia, Laos, and North Vietnam to carry out intelligence gathering or raiding missions on the enemy's 'home ground'; gathering intelligence about POWs and carrying out rescue missions when possible; rescuing downed aircrews in enemy territory ('Bright Light' missions); training, inserting, and controlling agents in North Vietnam to gather intelligence or form resistance groups; carrying out 'black' Psy Ops such as operating fake broadcasting stations inside North Vietnam; kidnapping or assassinating key enemy personnel; retrieving sensitive documents or equipment lost in enemy territory or in enemy hands; and inserting rigged mortar rounds or other booby-trapped ordnance in enemy arms caches (OPERATION ELDEST SON).

Among SOG special missions were those carried out under the code name OPERATION SHINING BRASS against NVA infiltration routes in Laos. Carried out by twelve man teams (three Americans and nine *Yards* or *Nungs*), SHINING BRASS missions were primarily intended to locate targets for bombing or for gunship ('Spooky,' 'Spectre,' etc) attacks, but sometimes reaction forces were called in after contact was made by the recon team.

SHINING BRASS missions were normally limited to areas near the Vietnamese/Laotian border, but later other special missions into Laos were carried out by Mobile Launch Team-3 from Nakhon Phanom, Thailand. Similar cross border reconnaissance operations were carried out into Cambodia. Between 1965 and 1972, a total of 2,675 cross border operations were carried out with a total of 103 US Special Forces casualties on such missions. *Indig* casualties were much higher. The relatively low number of US casualties should not be considered an indication of lack of danger, however; these missions were highly dangerous, but the US troops assigned to SOG were of such high caliber that they took lighter casualties than troops with lesser training would have taken. Nevertheless, some reconnaissance teams were never heard from again, seeming to have disappeared

General Abrams meets with US and Vietnamese personnel at MACV/SOG Command Control North (CCN) at DaNang during 1970. The beret badge of the ARVN officer at the left indicates that he is assigned to an airborne unit rather than an LLDB unit. (Larry Greene and Society of Vietnamese Rangers)

from the face of the earth, and others took very heavy casualties.

SOG's headquarters was located in Saigon near Tan Son Nhut Air Base. But while missions were normally planned at SOG HQ, missions were normally implemented or 'launched' from forward sites known as Forward Operations Bases (FOBs), later called Command and Control sites. Somtimes special missions were launched by 'Mobile Launch Teams', such as the one mentioned earlier at Nakhon Phanom. FOB-1 was located at Ban Me Thuot, FOB-2 at Kontum, FOB-3 at Khe Sanh, and FOB-4 at Da Nang.

Three 'Command and Control' units were formed in November of 1967, succeeding and consolidating the four FOBs.

Command and Control North (CCN) based at *Da Nang*, coordinated missions into Laos and North Vietnam (including 'Kit-Cat' missions deep in North Vietnam). Laos missions fell under OPERATION SHINING BRASS and PRAIRIE FIRE, while missions into North Vietnam were usually under OPERATION PLAN 34A. CCN was the largest of the Command and Control, with 'launch' sites at *Hue-Phu Bai, Khe Sanh, Quan Tri*, and *Kham Duc*.

Command and Control Central based at *Kontum*, carried out missions in the area where the borders of South Vietnam, Cambodia, and Laos meet.

Command and Control South (CCS) at *Ban Me Thout* was the smallest of the three Command and Control units and controlled missions into Cambodia.

CCN, CCC, and CCS were organized along similar lines. Their primary operational element was the Spike Reconnaissance Team, each consisting of three US Special Forces and nine indigenous personnel. These Reconnaissance Teams (RTs) were named primarily after states or snakes, although the RTs assigned to CCS tended to be named after implements or things relating to the weather. The total number of RTs available at SOG's peak was around seventy. Hatchet Forces backed up the RTs. Consisting of five US Special Forces and thirty *indigs*, Hatchet Forces were assigned missions requiring more men than were available in an RT. Hatchet Forces, for example, specialized in ambushing NVA or VC troops infiltrating into South Vietnam. Search-Locate-Annihilate-Mission (SLAM) companies acted as a reaction force for the RTs or were inserted to exploit RT information or situations. The three Command and Control units were shut down in March of 1971, being replaced by Task Force 1 Advisory Element at Da Nang until MACV/SOG was deactivated in April of 1972. Despite this deactivation, during April of 1972 many former SOG troopers were rushed back to Vietnam to help call in air strikes or carry out special missions in I Corps Tactical Zone during the Easter Invasion of South Vietnam. Certain special operations continued under the Technical Directorate Assistance Team 158, which was activated on 1 May 1972 as the successor to SOG. This unit operated until 12 March 1973 when it was deactivated. Officially this ended US special operations in Vietnam, but reportedly, certain US special operations personnel remained active in South Vietnam until after the fall of Saigon, and substantially beyond!

RECONNAISSANCE TEAMS KNOWN TO HAVE BEEN ASSIGNED TO A SPECIFIC COMMAND AND CONTROL

CCN	CCC	CCS
RT Adder	RT Alabama	RT Fork
RT Alaska	RT Arizona	RT Lightning
RT Anaconda	RT Arkansas	RT Mike Facs
RT Asp	RT California	RT Plane
RT Bushmaster	RT Colorado	RT Spike
RT Connecticut	RT Delaware	RT Trowel
RT Crusader	RT Hotcake	RT Weather
RT Hawaii	RT Illinois	
RT Hunter	RT Iowa	
RT Idaho	RT Kentucky	
RT Indiana	RT Montana	
RT Intruder	RT Nevada	
RT Kansas	RT New Mexico	
RT Krait	RT Texas	
RT Louisiana	RT Vermont	
RT Mamba	RT Washington	
RT Mississippi	RT West Virginia	
RT Missouri		
RT Moccasin		
RT New Jersey		
RT North Carolina		
RT Ohio		
RT Rhode Island		
RT Rattler		
RT Sidewinder		
RT Viper		
RT Virginia		
RT Wasp		

(Above) MACV/SOG Reconnaissance Team prior to a mission out of MLT-1 at Phu Bai during 1970. Team members are armed with CAR-15s and wear the Maguire (also known as STABO) rig for helicopter extraction while leaving the arms free to operate weapons if necessary. The use of Olive Drab towels or scarves as headgear was common among SOG personnel. Other than the American at right the members of this team are obviously *Nung* Chinese. (Don Valentie/Society of Vietnamese Rangers)

RANDALL Model 14 Attack Knife

Heavy brass guard with a 7 1/2 inch blade and a plastic Micarta handle.

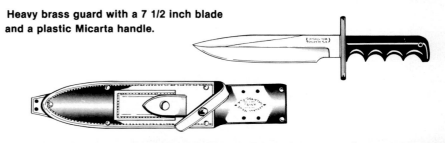

(Right) US advisors to the Quang Tin Province PRUs along with a field expedient coastal patrol craft assembled by the advisors. Tiger stripes (with the exception of the man on the right) and Green berets are worn.

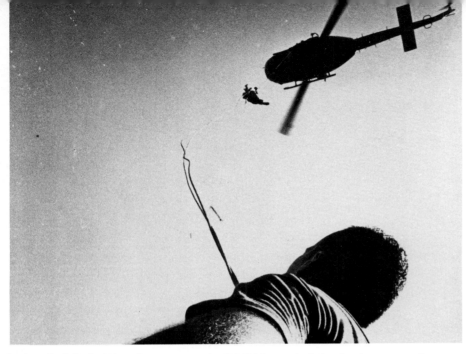

During the fall of 1968 an instructor at the MACV Recondo School acts as an anchor man while a student makes his first descent from a UH-1D Huey helicopter. (US Army)

A MACV Recondo School instructor discusses the drop with a student who has just descended from the 40 foot tower during a fall of 1968 course. Gloves and the ubiquitous 'boonie hat' are worn by the student, who is most likely a LRRP from one of the divisions or brigades. (US Army)

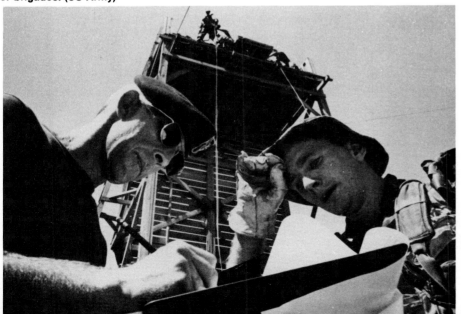

A student at the MACV Recondo School at Nha Trang begins his descent from a UH-1D Huey during his training in the fall of 1968. This student is wearing tiger stripes and carries full equipment. The use of full equipment was typical of the Recondo School which stressed realistic training including field exercises which often resulted in VC contacts. (US Army)

The Son Tay Raid

In May of 1970, Special Assistant for Counterinsurgency and Special Activities (SACSA) Brigadier General Donald Blackburn got the go-ahead from the Joint Chiefs of Staff (JCS) to begin planning a rescue mission into North Vietnam to free POWs believed to be held at Son Tay Prison located twenty-three miles from Hanoi. By 5 June 1970, a briefing had been given the Joint Chiefs about a possible rescue mission. Within a few days, Blackburn was given the go-ahead to continue planning the raid, and on 10 July Blackburn received the OK from the Joint Chiefs to implement his recommendation.

Originally, General Blackburn had wanted to lead the raid himself, however, his knowledge of sensitive intelligence matters automatically precluded him. Instead, the assignment went to Colonel 'Bull' Simons, a highly experienced Special Forces officer who had served under Blackburn with MACV/SOG. The raiding party commanded by Simons was code named 'Joint Contingency Task Group' (JCTG), and the mission was code named 'Ivory Coast'. For training JCTG personnel an area of Eglin Air Force Base was set aside. Air Force Brigadier General Leroy Manor, CO of Air Force special operations assets at Eglin AFB, was put in overall command, while his deputy, Col 'Bull' Simons, would lead the actual raid.

Since the optimum time for the raid appeared to be between 20 and 25 October, both men immediately began selecting their teams — Manor the air and planning elements and Simons the raiding force. At Fort Bragg, hundreds of Special Forces soldiers volunteered for the JCTG knowing only that it was 'hazardous' and the 'Bull' would be commanding. Fifteen officers and eighty-two NCOs, primarily from the 6th and 7th SFGs, were selected, from which the assault force, their backups, and support personnel would be chosen. A mock-up of the Son Tay Compound was built at Eglin for training. So Soviet spy satellites could not reveal its presence, the mock-up was designed to be dismantled during the day and quickly set up at night for training. Since the raid itself would be at night, training on the mock-up was at night. A $60,000 table top model of the camp was also built which included the capability of viewing the model under different types of lighting to duplicate moonlight, flares, etc.

Training of the raiding force began on 9 September 1970. Intensive training was given in night firing, hand signals, immediate action drills, house clearing, radio procedures, emergency medical techniques, and other skills already possessed to a greater or lesser degree by the raiders, who were highly trained Special Forces troops. The assault force was formed into three groups — the compound assault force of fourteen men who would actually land inside the prison compound; the command and security staff of twenty men; and the support group of twenty-two men. Simons himself commanded the support group. Beginning on 28 September the assault force practiced the actual assault with the Air Force crews who would fly the helicopters and other aircraft. The landing and assault were rehearsed again and again with many being 'live fire' run throughs. Alternative plans were also practiced in case one of the three teams failed to make it to the target.

On 27 October, Blackburn got the go ahead to begin moving personnel to Southeast Asia in preparation for the mission. On 1 November 1970 Blackburn and Simons, among others, left for Southeast Asia to lay the groundwork for the raid. By 12 November, both Blackburn and Simons were back in the States as the raiding force prepared to head for Thailand. On 18 November the President gave the 'GO' order for the raid; the raiders had left for Takhli RTAFB, Thailand a few hours previously in anticipation of receiving permission to carry out the raid. The weather had to be right for the operation to have a reasonable chance of success, and there had to be a one-quarter to three-quarter moon so the raiders would have acceptable light on the ground. Conditions were deemed acceptable to launch the raid on the night of 20/21 November.

On the evening of 20 November the raiders were shuttled to Udorn RTAFB from where the raid would be launched at 2318 local time. To create a diversion while the raid was underway, carrier based naval aircraft would be sent over Hanoi during the early hours of 21 November.

A student from Company L (Ranger), 75th Infantry, 101st Airborne Division ties a Claymore mine on a tree to clear a landing site on Hon Tri Island during a training exercise at the MACV Recondo School. (US Army)

At about 0218, Hanoi time, 21 November, the raid itself began. As a C-130 Hercules flare ship illuminated the area with flares, an HH-53, codenamed 'Apple Three,' opened up on the guard towers on Son Tay Prison with twin Gatling guns, bringing them crashing down.

Shortly thereafter, the HH-3 carrying the assault party landed inside the prison compound. A few minutes later the command and security group landed just outside the prison's walls. The support group led by Simons himself, however, had landed some 400 meters off course at what was labeled on the raiders' maps as a 'secondary school'. Instead of a secondary school they found themselves outside a barracks housing Chinese or Soviet advisors to the NVA, hundreds of whom Simons and his men killed within minutes of touching down, not only making them 'good Communists' but preventing them from reinforcing the Son Tay guards. Within ten minutes Simons had mopped up and had his men re-embarked and lifted to the Son Tay compound where they helped the assault and security elements eliminate dozens of guards at the prison.

Despite the smoothness of the assault, however, the raiders discovered that there were no POWs. They had been moved elsewhere. Less than thirty minutes after the raid began, the raiders were back in their choppers and heading back to Thailand. Only one raider had been wounded and he only slightly. The raid had gone perfectly, even Simon's landing at the wrong complex having proven fortuitous. However, the whole reason for the raid had been to free POWs, and there were no POWs. The Son Tay Raid, despite some press reports to the contrary, was not a failure; it was a huge success. It proved graphically to the North Vietnamese that they were vulnerable to attacks on installations at home. As a result, they had to tie up thousands of troops guarding installations within North Vietnam. They also lost credibility with the Chinese. Indirectly, the raid also led to improved treatment for American POWs. It should not be forgotten, either, that Simons' party of fifty-six raiders had killed over 200 of the enemy, many of them foreign advisors, without taking a

A pair of students at MACV Recondo School remain alert while waiting for exfiltration after a three day operation on Hon Tri Island in the Bay of Nha Trang. Such operations were a standard part of Recondo training and often resulted in enemy contacts. (US Army)

single loss themselves. Some estimates of the number killed run much higher. The Special Forces men and the Air Force and Navy pilots supporting them had done their jobs perfectly. It was a classic raid — in suddenly, hit hard, get out fast — but the intelligence had been wrong, a failure which points up the fact that intelligence is critical to special operations, especially raids into enemy territory. Who knows what might have happened if politicians in the United States would have had the courage to use this kind of weapon to its fullest.

46th Special Forces Company (Airborne) and UITG/FANK

During the Vietnam War, Special Forces personnel were engaged in training troops for other Southeast Asian countries. Company D, 1st Special Forces Group (Airborne) arrived in Thailand in October of 1966, to train Thai troops in counterinsurgency and conventional military skills. On 15 April 1967 the 46th Special Forces Company (Airborne) was activated using personnel of Company D, 1st SFG (Abn). Among the duties of the 46th Company was training the Royal Thai Regiment for deployment to Vietnam in September of 1967. By early 1968 the 46th Special Forces Company (Abn) had an authorized strength of369 personnel and was assigned to *Lopburi*. Its B-Detachments were at *Muang Sakon Nakhon, Pakchong*, and *Ban Kachon*. Frequently the A-Detachments were split among villages along the Northeastern border of Thailand where they helped with civic action and with anti-Communist-guerrilla activities. On 31 March 1972, HHD, 3rd Battalion, 1st SFG (Abn) was formed from the 46th Special Forces Company. This unit remained in Thailand helping prepare the Thais to defend themselves from Communist insurgencies until April of 1974.

US Army Vietnam Individual Training Group (VITG), formed of US Army Special Forces instructors, was established in South Vietnam on 1 November 1970 to train troops of the *Republique Khymer* (Cambodia). Training lasted for fifteen weeks and stressed light infantry skills. Training centers were at *Long Hai, Chi Lang, Dong Ba Thin,* and *Phuoc Tuy*. In May of 1972, this unit's designation was changed to Forces Armee Nationale Khmer (FANK). As of 30 December 1972 the unit was deactivated.

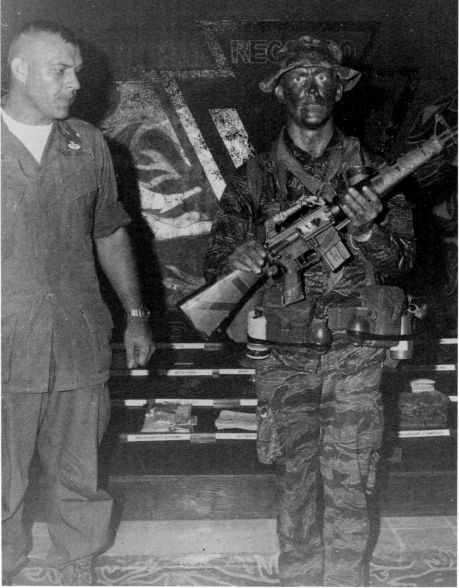

(Above) During March of 1969 a Special Forces instructor from the 5th SFG (Abn) assigned to the MACV Recondo School explains a student's equipment during a training lecture. The rifle is camouflaged and Black tape is used to keep grenades and other equipment secure and quiet.

(Left) A US advisor to the Vietnamese Hac Bao (Black Panther) Strike Company, an elite unit of the 1st ARVN Infantry Division looks over captured weapons with an Australian advisor. Note the Black beret.

LRRPs and Rangers

Shortly after the commitment of conventional ground combat units to Vietnam in 1965, division and brigade commanders realized they needed specific intelligence about their areas of operation. Normal intelligence channels were more concerned with the 'big picture' and the intelligence supplied was usually outdated. As a result, experienced combat veterans from the divisions and brigades — chosen for their skill in the bush, their alertness, their patrolling ability, and their willingness to volunteer for dangerous missions — were formed into Long Range Reconnaissance Patrols (LRRPs, pronounced *lirps*) or later LRPs (Long Range Patrols, still pronounced *lirps*). Originally created on a provisional basis, they were normally of platoon strength or less.

At first, LRRPs received no special training, but in September of 1966, the Reconnaissance/Commando (Recondo) School was established at Nha Trang, and many LRRPs were sent to this school for training. Included in the curriculum were those skills most applicable to small unit clandestine patrols in hostile territory, which included survival, field medicine, land navigation, silent movement, photography, communications, helicopter insertion and extraction, and escape and evasion.

But while tactics were being taught at the Recondo School they were also evolving in the field. Small teams — usually of four men — proved most effective. Normally, the four man team was organized with a point man, a team leader, a radioman, and a rearguard ('tailgunner'). Alertness and silence were absolute necessities for the LRRPs when on an operation since they were too few to engage in a pitched battle. LRRPs generally slept in shifts with equipment loosened, but still tight enough to move out immediately. When a team stopped, they automatically assumed defensive positions covering 360 degrees. To insure silent movement, sling swivels were removed from weapons, and equipment was taped to deaden any sound of metal or plastic. Camouflage tape was applied to weapons and equipment, and exposed skin was camouflaged. Since silence was so critical, communication when on patrol was normally through hand signals, taps on the shoulder, notes on paper (which was not discarded where the enemy might find it), or whispers directly into the ear. Radio communications were as silent as possible via pushing the radio talk button in a series of coded clicks. Aircraft flying in the vicinity monitored these calls in case emergency extraction was necessary or to relay messages.

As much as possible, LRRPs avoided contact with the enemy. Their primary job was intelligence gathering rather than combat. If LRRPs discovered an enemy unit, they often called in artillery fire, helicopter gunships, or tactical air support to destroy an enemy. Airmobile infantry might also be called in as a reaction unit once the LRRPs had located the enemy. While on patrol LRRPs kept their weapons ready in case combat could not be avoided, and if they had to fight they hit hard, fast, and first, trying to kill every enemy so that there would be none left to pursue them or to alert larger units. Occasionally, the LRRPs found themselves in a running firefight as they attempted to fight their way to a point where they could be extracted by chopper.

In very special situations LRRPs sometimes acted as the hunters rather than the hunted. When specific intelligence might be gained by 'snatching' a member of the local VC cadre, for example, LRRPs might carry out such an operation. More likely, however, they carried out hunter/killer operations in which they would set ambushes along VC trail networks. These ambushes made highly effective use of interlocking fields of fire, Claymore mines, and detonating cord in ditches along the side of the trail to catch any VC who dived for cover. Many LRRPs were trained as snipers and would eliminate enemy troops from a distance and then fade back into the bush.

The LRRPs' weapons reflected their need for firepower and compactness. The XM177E2 short version of the M-16 rifle was probably the most popular weapon, though standard M-16s and M-16s equipped with the M203 40MM grenade launcher also saw wide usage. Less commonly encountered were the M2 .30 caliber Carbine, M3 'Grease Gun', or 12 gauge Ithaca or Remington shotgun. The shotgun would normally be used by a point-man for rapidly clearing a trail should he encounter the enemy at close range. Occasional-

During the mid-1960s two US Ranger advisors to the Vietnamese Rangers, the *Biet Dong Quan* (BDQ) take part in a briefing. (US Army)

During the mid-1960s a US advisor to the Vietnamese Rangers observes hand-to-hand combat training. The advisor wears the Maroon beret of the Rangers and a Ranger pocket patch on his right breast pocket. At this time quite a bit of leeway was allowed in personal weapons, hence the Colt or Smith & Wesson magnum revolver on his hip. (US Army)

ly the AK-47 was used, however most LRRPs avoided it because of its distinctive sound which would immediately draw fire from any US troops in the vicinity. However, when operating in enemy territory where ammo resupply might be difficult, the AK-47 was occasionally chosen. Whatever weapon they chose LRRPs would carry as much ammo as possible. As many as thirty magazines might be carried in bandoliers and pouches. Additional weapons included various sidearms and a good supply of grenades — M26A1s, M34 'Willie Petes', and M18 'smokes'. Claymore mines were carried for use in protecting LRRPs at night, or when setting ambushes, though LRRPs also liked the Claymore because it was a ready source of C4 explosives, useful for everything from boobytraps to rapidly heating rations.

Since they operated in enemy controlled territory, rations and water were also problems for LRRPs. Eventually, special freeze-dried LRRP rations were developed, but they took a great deal of water. As a result a trademark of the LRRP — along with a lot of ammo — was a lot of canteens. In the early part of the war LRRPs generally wore the standard Green jungle utilities sometimes dyed black. Tiger stripe camouflage utilities were popular when they could be obtained in American sizes. Some LRRPs made their own by painting stripes on green utilities. While a Black beret was occasionally worn by the LR-RPs, it was rarely seen on operations. Flop or 'boonie' hats were worn, or just an OD scarf or towel was used as a head cover. Special 'boonie' hats with a large Orange dot on the interior were used by LRRPs and other special operations troops so that the Orange part could be turned out to help a chopper pilot spot them for extraction. Many LRRPs also wore pieces of NVA/VC equipment so their profile would not be obviously American if spotted along a trail.

By late 1967 the Long Range Reconnaissance Patrols (LRRPs) were known as Long Range Patrols (LRPs) and had become more formalized in their organization. Each division now had a LRP company assigned as follows:

1st Air Cav	Company E,	52nd Infantry	(LRP)
1st Infantry Division	Company F,	52nd Infantry	(LRP)
4th Infantry Division	Company E,	20th Infantry	(LRP)
	Company E,	58th Infantry	(LRP)
9th Infantry Division	Company E,	50th Infantry	(LRP)
23rd Infantry Division	Company E,	51st Infantry	(LRP)
25th Infantry Division	Company F,	50th Infantry	(LRP)
101st Airborne Division	Company F,	58th Infantry	(LRP)

The 199th Infantry Brigade (Light) also had Company F, 51st Infantry (LRP) assigned. The 11th Infantry Brigade and the 173rd Airborne Brigade each had a smaller sixty-one man detachment. US Army Vietnam had two of these smaller detachments assigned as well, while HQ of 2nd Field Force had Company D, 151st Infantry (LRP) assigned directly to it. This last unit was an Indiana National Guard unit which had volunteered for service in Vietnam.

As of 1 January 1969, the 75th Infantry, which traced its lineage to the World War II deep penetration unit, Merrill's Marauders, was reactivated as the parent unit of all LRP companies, now designated as Ranger infantry companies. However, since the Ranger Department wanted to maintain the high standards associated with the term 'Ranger', it was stipulated, that only those men who had completed Ranger training could wear the Ranger arc.

Each of these new Ranger companies was standardized at a strength of 118 men (three officers and 115 enlisted). It was organized into a company HQ of one officer and seventeen enlisted men, and two fifty man platoons. The basic element of each platoon was a six man patrol. These Ranger companies assigned to brigades were normally only half-companies of sixty men. Ranger companies were assigned as follows:

1st Air Cav	Company H,	75th Infantry	(Ranger)
1st Infantry Division	Company I,	75th Infantry	(Ranger)
4th Infantry Division	Company K,	75th Infantry	(Ranger)
1st Brigade, 5th Infantry Division (Mechanized)	Company P,	75th Infantry	(Ranger)
9th Infantry Division	Company E,	75th Infantry	(Ranger)
23rd Infantry Division	Company G,	75th Infantry	(Ranger)
25th Infantry Division	Company F,	75th Infantry	(Ranger)
3rd Brigade, 82nd Airborne Division	Company O,	75th Infantry	(Ranger)
101st Airborne Division	Company L,	75th Infantry	(Ranger)
173rd Airborne Brigade	Company N,	75th Infantry	(Ranger)
199th Infantry Brigade (Light)	Company M,	75th Infantry	(Ranger)
I Field Force	Company C,	75th Infantry	(Ranger)
II Field Force	Company D,	75th Infantry	(Ranger)

US Ranger advisor to the BDQ wears the well-known Viet Ranger helmet cover and leaf pattern utilities. (Don Valentine)

In addition to carrying out the long range patrol mission, Rangers also served as the brigade or divisional reaction force and often supplied personnel for special missions.

Many other Rangers served in Vietnam. Graduates of Ranger training were spread throughout units in Vietnam where their knowledge of jungle survival techniques and patrolling proved invaluable. Approximately 2,000 Rangers also acted as advisors to the Vietnamese Rangers — the Biet Dong Quan. US Rangers had helped establish the Vietnamese ranger training centers at Trung Lap, Tet Son, and Duc My, and continued to serve in the field with BDQ battalions. By the end of the war, almost 300 US Rangers had been either killed in action or were missing in action.

While the contributions of LRRPs and Rangers in Vietnam did not receive the publicity which accompanied those of the Special Forces, their value was incalculable.

During July of 1968 a LRRP from the 9th Infantry Division checks his URC-10 emergency radio, which was widely used by Special Forces, LRRPs, and Rangers. He wears slant pocket jungle utilities and the Black beret sometimes seen on LRRPs in Vietnam. The MACV Recondo School pocket patch on his left pocket indicates his graduation from the Recondo training course. (US Army)

During May of 1970 a LRRP of Company D (Ranger), 75th Infantry assigned to II Field Force acts as point man for his patrol. (US Army)

(Above Right) In May of 1970, members of the Long Range Patrol from Company D (Ranger), 75th Infantry report to their team leader after a reconnaissance of the area. An Olive Drab scarf is worn as a sweatband by the LRP on the left. Sweatbands were widely worn by LRRPs and anyone else carrying out long range patrol missions. (US Army)

Browning 9mm Mk 1 Pistol
Carried by MACV/SOG Recon Teams

(Right) A LRRP of Company D (Ranger), 75th Infantry prepares to detonate a Claymore mine in response to movement he has heard along a trail. The fact that he is armed with the M-79 grenade launcher is a bit unusual since LRRPs were normally armed with a M-16 mounting a M203 grenade launcher, however, most LRRPs were allowed to exercise a good bit of leeway in armament selection. (US Army)

**75th Infantry (Ranger)
Beret Flash**

SEALS

The Navy's SEALs were formed in 1962 after the Vietnam conflict was already attracting the attention of the US armed forces. Trained to operate in all three mediums, Sea, Air, and Land — from which they took their name. The SEALs were the Navy's counterinsurgency and special warfare experts. To help counter the strong VC presence in the Mekong Delta and to supply combat swimmers to MACV/SOG and other operations the first SEAL detachments were deployed to Vietnam in 1966.

Each SEAL Team consisted of a little under 200 men with the primary tactical unit being a three man fire element. Both SEAL Team One and SEAL Team Two would see service in Vietnam. One of the first missions assigned to the SEALs was setting up observation and listening posts along suspected VC infiltration routes on the waterways and trails crisscrossing the Mekong Delta. After identifying routes and bases SEALs mounted raids to ambush the VC and destroy their bases. These reconnaissance missions proved immediately successful and their number was expanded, some observation teams staying in place for a week at a time.

SEAL patrols ranged widely on hunter-killer missions, especially in the Rung Sat Special Zone south of Saigon. Three man SEAL teams were inserted in the swampy areas of the Rung Sat by means of 'Mike' boats, and would then walk and/or swim to a point where they could possibly observe the VC, and if the opportunity arose ambush them. On such operations, SEALs usually maintained complete silence. Relying instead on operational experience together and supplemented by hand signals when needed, SEALs moved silent and deadly through the Delta. Using Claymore mines and demo cord, the SEALs would often lay booby-traps along VC trails. A variation of this technique was to set an ambush and to booby trap any likely escape routes from the killing zone.

Later in the war 'Boston Whalers' were used to insert SEAL teams. These 16 foot fiberglass boats had a very shallow draft and were well suited for operations in the Delta. The IBS (Inflatable Boat, Small) was also available, though it was used more often for clandestine insertions from submarines along the North Vietnamese coast. Whatever type of craft was used for the insertion, as soon as the SEALs were dropped off, the boat would immediately move downstream so the position of the team was not compromised. SEALs were also inserted by the choppers of Naval Light Helicopter Attack Squadrons. In some cases SEALs dove directly into the water from the chopper, then swimming to their objective.

In 1966 the SEALs, as well as the Army's Special Forces, had become involved in the ICEX (Intelligence and Exploitation) program which was aimed at identifying and neutralizing the VC infrastructure within South Vietnam. Working both with ICEX and independently, SEALs killed or captured numerous VC, unearthed arms and supply caches, and acted as spearheads or scouts for South Vietnamese or American units operating in the Delta. SEALs assigned to MACV/SOG were used for missions into Haiphong Harbor and other points inside of North Vietnam, and as the war intensified, critical bridges along supply routes in North Vietnam were often targeted for SEAL demolition raids as well.

By 1967, as a result of the success of the SEALs in the Delta region, their numbers in-country were increased substantially. Their major base was at *Nha Be*, and SEALs maintained mobile bases on barges on the waterways of the Delta. From these mobile bases SEALs mounted hunter-killer and intelligence missions throughout the region. Occasionally SEALs were called upon to act as underwater demolition specialists when it was necessary to clear the waterways. When large scale Riverine operations were mounted SEALs frequently acted as scouts. Two good examples are CRIMSON TIDE in September of 1967, and BOLD DRAGON III in March of 1968. In addition to acting as scouts during these OPERATIONS the SEALs also blew up a number of enemy installations. During BOLD DRAGON III SEALs hit *Tanh Dinh* Island especially hard, blowing up numerous VC bunkers and destroying a VC weapons factory. In OPERATION CHARLESTON SEALs acted on intelligence from captured VC documents to hit VC wells and supply sources in the Rung Sat Special Zone.

Navy SEALs practice helicopter insertions by rapelling to the beach at their base at Nha Be during January of 1967. (US Navy)

A landing craft crew awaits the return of a SEAL team they have placed ashore during OPERATION CRIMSON TIDE on the Bassac River in the Mekong Delta during September of 1967. (US Navy)

Late in 1967 the Phoenix Program was initiated as a successor to ICEX. A key element in the Phoenix Program was the PRUs (pronounced *Prews*) — the Provincial Reconnaissance Units — elite professional strike forces drawn from local MIKE Forces and the *Chieu Hoi* (Communist turncoats), and other sources. Along with Army Special Forces, SEALs acted as advisors to the PRUs. Working as the Phoenix Program's 'direct action' arm, the PRUs operated in ten to twenty man teams under Special Forces or SEAL advisors carrying out reconnaissance, intelligence, ambush, 'snatch', or assassination missions against VC political cadre, tax collectors, or sympathizers. Due to the training and assistance provided by SEALs and other US advisors, the Phoenix Program was especially effective in the Mekong Delta.

SEALs also acted as advisors and trainers to their Vietnamese counterparts — the *Lin Dei Nugel Nghai* (LLDN). Working alongside the LLDN, SEALs coordinated many joint operations, including raids on small VC POW compounds in the Delta. On 22 November 1970, fifteen SEALs and nineteen Vietnamese successfully attacked such a VC camp.

SEALs were also assigned special security duties around US port facilities including patrols to prevent the infiltration of enemy swimmers. At Cam Ranh Bay SEALs worked with attack-trained dolphins to thwart enemy attacks on US shipping.

To carry out their special missions SEALs were equipped with a lot of special hardware unique to themselves. Their armory included the 5.56MM Stoner M63A1 light machine gun, the Ithaca M37 12 gauge shotgun, the H&K G3 assault rifle, and the 9MM Smith & Wesson Mark 22 Model O silenced pistol. Known as the 'Hush Puppy' Mark 22 had been developed for eliminating enemy sentry dogs. In Vietnam the Mark 22 also was used for silently eliminating VC or NVA. The SEALs were also equipped with more standard arms such as the M60 GPMG (in some cases cut down, lightened versions), M16, and XM177E2 rifles. A typical SEAL three man fire element would be armed with an Ithaca Model 37, an M-16 with M203 40MM grenade launcher attached, and an M63A1.

It is generally stated that the SEALs had been withdrawn from Vietnam by late 1971 or early 1972, but there are indications that at least a few SEALs were in-country and involved in special operations after these dates. During the war SEALs accounted for 580 confirmed kills and over 300 probable kills. These numbers are, no doubt, low since MACV/SOG and Phoenix 'kills' attributable to the SEALs aren't likely to have been counted. Because of their ability to attack so suddenly and silently and with such ferocity, SEALs were certainly among the US troops most feared by the VC and NVA. And that fear was well founded.

Smith & Wesson Military Mark 22 Model 0 9mm "Hush Puppy" Pistol

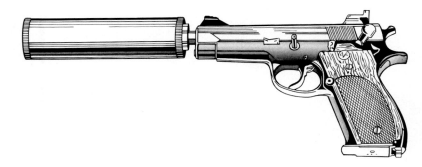

During September of 1967 SEALs return to base after OPERATION CRIMSON TIDE. M-60 GPMGs are mounted on each side of the boat. The round object on the left side of each of the M-60s is a tin can which was used to guide the ammunition belt more reliably. (US Navy)

(Below) SEAL laying down suppressing fire along the shore as the 'Mike' boat in which he is riding heads back to their base at *Nha Be*. His 'boonie' hat is worn over a helmet and he is wearing a flak jacket. While carrying out operations ashore SEALs would usually dispense with the helmet and jacket. (US Navy)

During September of 1967 a SEAL waits in ambush during a hunter-killer mission in the Mekong Delta. The camouflage, which includes the distinctive SEAL face camouflage is obviously effective. The camouflage beret worn by this SEAL was widely worn by SEALs. In this case the beret is flopped over the left eye in the French/Vietnamese style rather than over the right eye in US style. (US Navy)

In September of 1967 a group of SEALs are being debriefed aboard a river patrol boat after a mission. Camo berets are worn by the two SEALs in the foreground. (US Navy)

During OPERATION CRIMSON TIDE in September of 1967 Navy SEALs destroy enemy fortifications along the Bassac River. (US Navy)

As their Mike Boat departs the SEALs watch the VC fortification they have just blown up burn during CRIMSON TIDE. September 1967 (US Navy)

In September of 1967 during a mission in the Mekong Delta a SEAL returns to his landing craft with a captured VC suspect. (US Navy)

Firing an M60 GPMG from the hip a SEAL lays down suppressive fire against the shoreline during extraction after a mission. (US Navy)

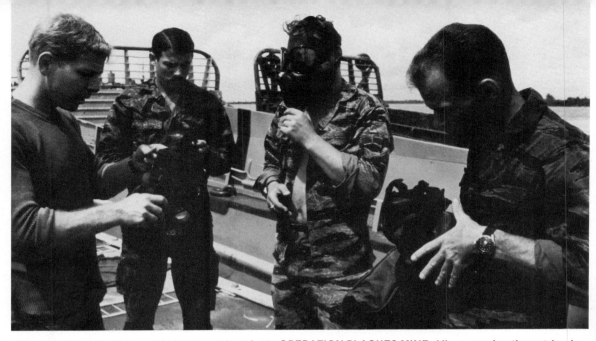

(Above) SEALs checking out their gas masks prior to OPERATION PLAQUES MINE. All are wearing tiger striped utilities and the SEAL on the right is wearing a dive watch. (US Navy)

(Above) During November of 1967 a member of SEAL Team One wearing a gas mask during rehearsals for OPERATION PLAQUES MINE in November of 1967. (US Navy)

(Left) Members of SEAL Team One climb aboard a craft of the Mobile Riverine Force after a mission in November of 1967. (US Navy)

A tired member of SEAL Team One after a mission during November of 1967. He is wearing a camouflaged beret and scarf. (US Navy)

(Above Right) During November of 1967 two Navy Gunners stand by a 57ᴍᴍ recoilless rifle in support of SEAL operations ashore. A telescopic sight has been rigged to their weapon. (US Navy)

(Right) During November of 1967 members of SEAL Team One move down the Bassac River in an assault boat. (US Navy)

SEAL Lt (jg) removes his 'boonie' hat after he is picked up following a mission along the Bassac River during November of 1967. (US Navy)

During January of 1968 a member of SEAL Team One undergoes tactical training in the desert of Southern California. He wears the leaf pattern camouflage which became available to elite units in Vietnam during 1968. (US Navy)

Seal Ammunition Carry Coats

Type I
Buoyant, Ammunition Carrying — Rifleman

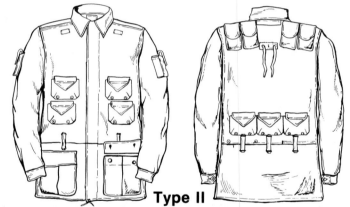

Type II
Buoyant, Ammunition Carrying — Grenadier

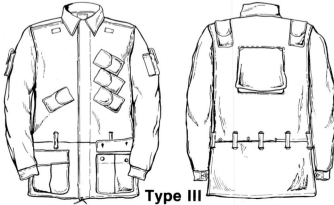

Type III
Buoyant, Ammunition Carrying — Radioman

In March of 1968 a SEAL sets demolition charges to destroy a VC bunker on Tanh Dinh Island during operation BOLD DRAGON III. A flak jacket is worn over his tiger stripes. (US Navy)

Members of a SEAL team check their weapons prior to insertion. Of special interest are the H&K G3 rifle carried by the SEAL the upper right and the grenadier's vest for 40MM grenades worn by the SEAL at the lower right. October 1968 (US Navy)

During March of 1968 SEALs are being ex-tracted under VC fire after blowing up enemy bunkers on Tanh Dinh Island as part of BOLD DRAGON III. The man on the right is providing cover fire with an M-79 grenade launcher. (US Navy)

SEALs man their weapons as they prepare to be inserted for a mission. (US Navy)

In April of 1968 a SEAL jumps ashore from a Boston Whaler in the Rung Sat Special Zone. (US Navy)

During October of 1968 a group of SEALs aboard a Riverine craft prepare to be in-serted. The SEAL in the center wears the Distinctive face camouflage patterns used by SEALs and carries additional M63A1 ammunition. (US Navy)

Stoner M63A1

A SEAL crouches behind cover during a training opera-tion. A 40mm grenade launcher is mounted below the bar-rel of the M-16. (US Navy)

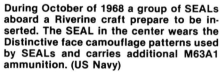

(Above) SEALs disembarking during a mission on Tanh Dinh Island in March of 1968. Already ashore are ARVN troops taking part in the mission. The lead SEAL in the water carries an M63A1 with a 150 round drum magazine. (US Navy)

(Above Right) SEAL Team being inserted for a mission via helicopter. (US Navy)

US Navy Underwater Knife

Blade is 7 1/4 inches long with saw teeth on the back edge. All metal parts are made of a non-magnetic, stain resistant, non-ferrous alloy. Sheath is made of a gray fiber glass.

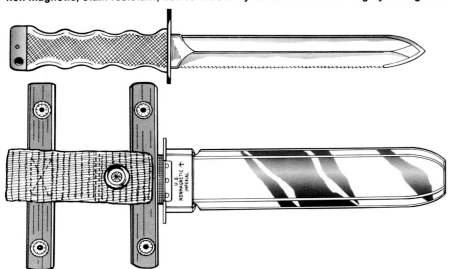

(Right) Navy Armored Troop Carrier of the type used by Riverine forces and which sometimes were used to insert SEALs passes under a fortified bridge on the *Bay Hap River* during April of 1970. (US Navy)

US Marine Corps Recons

Marine Recons are considered an elite among a force that already considers itself to be an elite force. Trained in airborne, helicopter, SCUBA, and small boat insertions; communications, long range patrolling, intelligence gathering, and other special operations skills; the Recons perform missions similar to the Army's LRRPs or Special Forces, and the Navy SEALs. While primarily an intelligence gathering unit, in Vietnam the Recons were used as raiders and advisors to CIDG units as well. Normally, divisional reconnaissance battalions were charged with missions in support of the divisions to which they were assigned, while Force Recon companies were assigned to pre-assault and post-assault reconnaissance in support of landing forces. Force Recons are believed to have been used along the North Vietnam coast line to evaluate possible sites for amphibious landings.

Marine Recons of the 1st Force Reconnaissance Company were among the earliest US combat troops in Vietnam when they carried out beach reconnaissance missions before the landing of the 9th Marine Expeditionary Brigade in March of 1965. During a later beach reconnaissance mission the 1st Force Recon Company took its first casualty when one of its men was killed in a clash with the VC.

Although 'deep reconnaissance' platoons of Marine Recon units can carry out missions up to 100 kilometers ahead of the unit to which they are assigned, in Vietnam most reconnaissance missions were carried out much closer to major units. During the early part of the Marine commitment, most Recon patrols consisted of twelve to twenty-four men, though later in the war smaller LRRP size units of four to six men were found to be more effective. A major limiting factor on the length of time that these early patrols could stay out was the short battery life and short range of the PRC-10 radio. Only a limited number of batteries, which died quickly in Vietnam, could be carried, but with the introduction of the PRC-25 with longer lasting batteries the length of patrols was increased by 1966.

During 1965 the 3rd Recon Battalion and 1st Force Recon Company arrived in-country, followed in 1966 by the 1st Recon Battalion, and in 1967 by the 3rd Force Recon Company. As of October 1965 the 1st Force Recon Company had a strength of nine officers and 103 enlisted men and was assigned to the 3rd Recon Battalion.

Late in 1965 the 2nd Platoon, 1st Force Recon Company was assigned to the Special Forces camp at *Ba To* and the 3rd Platoon, 1st Force Recon Company was assigned to the Special Forces camp at *Tra Bang*. Both platoons were to be used on 'Bird Watcher' deep penetration missions. Eventually Recons would operate in Laos and North Vietnam. Marine Recons were also assigned to MACV/SOG for cross border operations. An indication of the toughness of the Recons can be gained from the experience of one Recon Marine assigned to 'Bird Watcher' missions out of *Ba To*. Wounded and captured by the NVA, he escaped twice, the second time by forcing two NVA soldiers at knife point to carry him back to *Ba To*!

Recons were used for various other types of missions as well. In operations such as BLACK FERRET in November of 1965, for example, two platoons of the 1st Recon Battalion acted as screening units. Other Recons served as advisors to the CIDG in I Corps, and still others acted as quick response patrols providing security for downed Marine helicopters until they could be lifted out for salvage or repairs. While some of their assigned missions misused the Recons, who were intended for intelligence gathering, the Recons carried them out well. During 1965 Recon companies had the highest VC kill rate of any unit in-country. A more effective use of the Recon units was in 'Stingray' missions during which the Recons would locate enemy concentrations and call in air or artillery strikes. Recons were especially useful for patrols along the DMZ and in the hilly area north of *Hue* near the DMZ. It should be noted that Recon patrols often went north of the DMZ.

Throughout the siege of *Khe Sanh*, Recon units including Company B, 3rd Battalion, and 3rd Platoon, Company D, 3rd Recon Battalion were present, but they were used in reserve rather than as reconnaissance troops. Other Recon troops were used to deter-

During the fall of 1965 members of the 3rd Recon Battalion cross the Mong River during a sweep and clear mission. All are wearing standard USMC fatigue caps. (USMC)

mine NVA and VC strength, and to locate concentrations in other areas of I Corps, especially around *Hue* during the Tet Offensive, to which the Siege of *Khe Sanh* was a corollary. Recons were also involved in scouting and recon missions for other large-scale Marine operations. Elements of the 3rd Recon Battalion were used extensively in OPERATIONS KENTUCKY and SCOTLAND during 1968 and 1969 respectively.

The 3rd Recon Battalion left Vietnam during November of 1969, along with the 3rd Marine Division, and was followed in August of 1970 by the 3rd Force Recon Company. The 1st Recon Battalion left in March of 1971 with the 1st Marine Division, and was followed the next month by the 1st Force Recon Company. Recons had been assigned to MACV/SOG, especially CCN and the 'Maritime Studies Group' and a few may have stayed around with SOG until 1972 or later.

(Left) A USMC Recon wearing SCUBA gear for an underwater infiltration mission. Mid-1960 (USMC)

(Right) Two USMC Recons observe an enemy position while on a reconnaissance mission during the mid-1960s. Camouflage helmet covers are being worn as head gear. The Recon at the right carries a M3A1 SMG. (USMC)

USMC Recon Wings

(Below) USMC Recons on patrol near the Laotian border and the DMZ during 1967. They are wearing the ever popular 'boonie' hats and are heavily-laden for an extended patrol. (USMC)

Airforce Combat Control Teams And Combat Security Police

The Air Force had two units serving in Vietnam which should be classified as 'special forces' — the Combat Control Teams (CCTs) and the Combat Security Police (CSPs). And while the elite PJs of the Aerospace Rescue and Recovery Service were as much an elite unit as the CCTs or CSPs, the PJs' mission was to rescue downed airmen, and while this task often included missions behind enemy lines, it was not a 'special forces' mission within the parameters of this book.

Combat Control Teams

During the Vietnam War, the CCTs received their initial training at Sewart AFB, Arkansas. In addition to being trained as air traffic controllers and as parachutists, CCTs were also trained in communications, emergency first aid, patrol, ambush, and counter-ambush tactics, the establishment of drop zones and landing zones, and helicopter insertions and extractions. Combat Control Teams received more intensive weapons training than any other Air Force unit except the Combat Security Police.

CCTs assigned to aerial port detachments worked closely with the Army's Special Forces at Special Forces camps where the CCTs would guide transport aircraft to either land on the camp airstrip or drop supplies. CCTs also acted as pathfinders for airborne operations. In some situations CCTs called in air strikes to support Special Forces camps. It's believed that CCTs were used on clandestine missions along the Ho Chi Minh Trail and elsewhere to spot for USAF gunships such as 'Puff' or 'Spectre'. During the so-called siege at *Khe Sanh* CCTs marked drop zones or landing zones and also stood by to assume control of incoming C-123s and C-130s should the Marine control tower at *Khe Sanh* have lost radio contact.

Within South Vietnam CCTs originally came under the control of the Airlift Control Center (ALCC) at Tan Son Nhut, but after its activation in October of 1966, Combat Control Teams became part of the 834th Air Division. Individual Combat Control Teams were assigned to the three aerial port squadrons or the smaller aerial port detachments within the 834th Air Division.

In addition to their contribution to the defense of *Khe Sanh*, CCTs also played an important role in aerial supply efforts during the Tet Offensive, operations in Cambodia and Laos, and the 1972 Easter Invasion. These major operations, however, were only among the more visible CCT missions. Throughout the war in Southeast Asia at small airstrips at Special Forces 'fighting camps' all over Vietnam CCTs made sure that critical supplies made it through the pipeline.

Combat Security Police

The Air Force's other special operations unit came into existence as a result of VC attacks against US air bases. The Combat Security Police (CSP) were trained as Air Force 'Rangers' and were equipped to function as a quick reaction force should an air base come under attack, or as a seek and destroy unit which could set ambushes to destroy enemy infiltrators outside or on the perimeter of a base.

The forerunner of the Combat Security Police was the 1041st Security Police Squadron which received sixteen weeks of Ranger type training from Army Ranger instructors at Schofield Barracks, Hawaii as part of 'OPERATION SAFESIDE'.

As a result of the success of the 1041st Security Police Squadron during its tour in Vietnam, Combat Security Police Squadrons were formed and trained as an elite light infantry, combining the skills of the Army's Rangers and the British RAF Regiment. Each CSP

During August of 1968 members of the USAF 821st Combat Security Police (CSP) Squadron man a .50 caliber machine gun at Phan Rang Air Base. All are wearing the 'boonie' hat and camouflage utilities. (USAF)

squadron had an authorized strength of twenty-one officers and 538 enlisted men. The squadron was broken into three flights, each with six officers and 161 enlisted men. Each of these flights consisted of three field sections of one officer and thirty-two enlisted men and one support section of one officer and sixty-three enlisted men. These sections were broken into ten man fire teams. Between April of 1968 and February of 1971 three Combat Security Police Squadrons — the 821st, 822nd, and 823rd — served in Vietnam. Although each squadron was nominally assigned to Phan Rang Air Base during its tour in Vietnam, flights or even sections of the Combat Security Police Squadron were often sent elsewhere on special assignment.

During March of 1968 CCTs of the 8th Aerial Port Squadron prepare to use smoke grenades to signal transport aircraft the location of the drop zone for supplies at Khe Sanh. At Khe Sanh these CCTs wear the extra protection of helmets and flak jackets. (USAF)

USAF Combat Control Team Beret Badge
(Post Vietnam)

(Left) Two members of the 8th Aerial Port Squadron Combat Control Team (CCT) maintain radio contact with USAF transport aircraft delivering supplies to the Special Forces camp at *Cai Cai* during April of 1968. During the Vietnam War CCTs did not have a beret badge so they wore parachutist's wings on their Dark Blue berets. (USAF)

In October of 1969 CCTs help a C-130 Hercules take off from a landing strip. (USAF)

A CCT at Cai Cai Special Forces Camp directs in a C-130 delivering supplies to the camp.
April 1968 (USAF)